Building a Shelf and a Bike Rack

Ken Ainsworth

Illustrations by Tina Holdcroft

Photography by Rodrigo Moreno

Annick Press • Toronto • New York • Vancouver

 We acknowledge the support of the Canada Council for the Arts
for our publishing program. We also thank the Ontario Arts Council.

Cataloguing in Publication Data
Ainsworth, Ken, 1957-
        Building a shelf and a bike rack

(Building together ; 2)
ISBN 1-55037-555-5 (bound) ISBN 1-55037-513-X (pbk.)

1. Woodwork – Juvenile literature. 2. Shelving (Furniture) – Juvenile literature.
3. Bicycles – Equipment and supplies – Juvenile literature.
I. Holdcroft, Tina. II. Moreno, Rodrigo. III. Title.
IV. Series: Ainsworth, Ken, 1957–   . Building together ; 2.

TT185.A36 1998   j684'.08   C98-931295-X

The art in this book was rendered in watercolours.
The text was typeset in Times Roman and Officina Sans.

Distributed in Canada by: Published in the U.S.A. by Annick Press (U.S.) Ltd.
Firefly Books Ltd.   Distributed in the U.S.A. by:
3680 Victoria Park Avenue   Firefly Books (U.S.) Inc.
Willowdale, ON   P.O. Box 1338
M2H 3K1   Ellicott Station
                                 Buffalo, NY 14205

Printed and bound in Canada by Friesens.

Introduction

In the spring of 1994, my daughters and I gathered up some scrap wood and a few basic hand tools. I thought we'd see what we could come up with.

The flower Lindsey made sits beside Carly's "person" on my desk, and both have "Made in Childhood" stamped all over them—only a child could have worked the gleeful inexactness and the wonderfully rough cutting job. My daughters' joy in their work and our memories of building together provided the seedling from which the concept of this series grew.

These books aren't about making perfect objects from wood, or turning children into skilled woodworkers. They are about adults—with or without woodworking training—and children having fun together. My training actually got in the way at first. I had to learn that children are justifiably proud of work that to me still looks a bit rough, but now I love that mark of authenticity.

This is not to say that we adults can't sometimes step in and say, "Do you mind if I sand this a bit more?" Just don't take a power sander and grind away all the marks of the child's work. Sometimes it will be necessary to finish, or even do, some task that the child finds frustrating or too difficult. Even then, I try to keep in mind that it's the child's project and he or she needs to give permission before I can mess with it.

Before you start, it is important that you read the safety guidelines on page 4 and discuss them with the child you'll be working with.

The *Building Together* series is designed to be easy to follow for both adults and kids. Every photograph shows exactly how Lindsey and I did that step, and the instructions are like listening to our conversation as we worked. Sidebars give details about the skills needed for the steps on each page. (Note: We worked with hand tools for this series, since they are safer than power tools, readily available, relatively inexpensive, and satisfying to use.) Each book provides a miniature woodworking course, but feel free to do whichever projects you like—each one is self-contained. Most of all, have fun building together!

Ken Ainsworth

Contents

Page **5**

Page **15**

Safety

There is, of course, some risk involved in working with tools. Working safely is twofold: taking precautions to minimize risk and being careful while we are working.

Preparing the work area

Remember that children have not yet reached adult levels of co-ordination. They move differently, they are less cautious, and have sudden bursts of restless energy. With these things in mind:

● Store spare lumber well away from the work area. Leaning boards against the wall is okay as long as they are not too long or wobbly. Alternatively, lay them on the floor against the wall.

● Put away sharp tools as soon as you are finished using them. Never leave tools, pieces of wood, or other equipment lying around on tables, chairs, benches or floors, where people can step on them, trip over them or stumble against them.

● Whatever you decide to use as your "workbench" (see Tools and Materials, page 6), make sure that it is sturdy and won't collapse or tip over.

● Keep a bag of small wood scraps on hand for using as saw blocks, cutting guides and clamp pads. (For more information, see the Tools and Materials pages and sidebars on clamping.)

● Keep out small children and pets! You can't supervise the older child's woodworking and watch over a young child at the same time. A playful dog or cat can knock things over, jump onto work surfaces, and cause damage or harm to materials, people, and themselves.

Things to watch out for while working

Irritation and fatigue can greatly increase the risk of accidents. Be sure to take your time, set reasonable goals, limit the length of each session, and take frequent breaks when building together, especially if someone small *or* big gets frustrated or angry.

Children must always be supervised when woodworking, and both adults and children must follow some basic rules.

● Always wear safety glasses when you are sawing or hammering, or any time when little or big things might fly around and get into or near eyes.

● Wear dust masks to help keep sawdust and wood chips out of mouths and noses.

● Younger children should hold tools such as saws and hammers in both hands for added strength and control, and so that one hand doesn't get in harm's way. (See sidebars for more information.)

● Even sandpaper can cause injury. It tends to sand skin as well as wood, and the paper can pick up splinters, which then get stuck in fingers and hands.

● Children should never be allowed to run or jump around the work area.

● Both children and adults must wear sturdy footwear with thick uppers.

We all learn by making mistakes. The adult's job is doing everything possible to see that the learning process doesn't result in injury.

Bike Rack

Tools and Materials

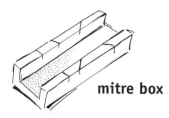

mitre box

measuring tape

8' of 4x4 (in pieces at least 4' long), and 64' of 2x2, pine, spruce, redwood, or cedar (we used spruce)

four or five large C-clamps, at least 5"

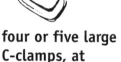

pencil

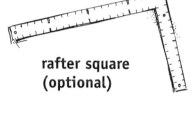

rafter square (optional)

try square (or any square a child can handle; see p. 12)

one backsaw or general purpose wood-cutting handsaw, plus one smaller saw (smaller saw optional)

two pairs strap-on safety goggles (one child-size, if possible)

100 2½" galvanized nails

hammer

Not shown: assorted wood scraps to use as saw blocks (see photos). You will need a traffic-free area, a safe place to put tools and materials when you've finished using them, and a bench, sturdy chair, picnic table, edge of a deck, or other suitable surface. If you are working with long pieces of wood, add another support of a similar height (see photo p. 8).

Most lumberyards use the imperial system of measurement. If you want to use metric, convert our measurements, factoring 2.54 centimetres per inch.

Illustrations not to scale

Names for tools can vary. If you are unsure about terms, ask at your local hardware store or lumberyard.

Lindsey's new bike was as shiny as a jewel. She didn't want to stop riding it when Dad called her in for supper. Even then, she kept finding excuses to get up from the table so she could look out the window and make sure it was okay.

Before bed, she carefully set the bike on its kick-stand and went inside. Next morning she found it lying on the ground. Dad came outside and looked it over. "I don't see any scratches, Lindsey. It was pretty windy last night. Maybe a bike rack would be a good idea."

You mean, we could build one?" said Lindsey.

"Sure."

"Okay," said Lindsey. "Can we start today?"

They measured their tires, and went inside to sketch some plans and make a shopping list.

 BIKE RACK

About wood

Boards are called "one by six" (1x6), "two by four" (2x4), etc. This refers to the size the board was when it was cut from the log. Smoothing and trimming at the sawmill make it slightly smaller.

Measuring

Before you start, measure your own bike tires to make sure our measurements will work for you.

Clamping

Clamp as shown (you might want to add more clamps), unless you are experienced. If you are, then clamp with your cutting line centred between the two chairs and stand well clear of the saw's path when you finish your cut— "follow-through" can cause injury.

Safety tip

Children should not handle 4x4—it's very heavy. If you need help, ask another adult.

1

Dad and Lindsey started with the frame. They measured 48" from the end of a piece of 4x4 and made a pencil mark. Then Lindsey used the small square to draw a cutting line across the wood. Dad turned the 4x4 so she could continue the line around all four sides.

2

Dad set the 4x4 across two sturdy old chairs. He and Lindsey clamped the wood to each chair, then added a second clamp on the far end. They clamped a saw block to the chair leg that was nearest the cutting line. It stuck out about 8".

BIKE RACK

3

Dad started sawing, leaning on the 4x4 to help keep it steady. When he was halfway through the cut, he and Lindsey loosened the clamps on the 4x4. Dad turned the wood over, reclamped it, and finished the cut from the other side. He did the other 4x4 the same way.

4

"We're going to cut the cross-pieces now, right, Dad?"
"That's right. They have to be 32" long."
They measured 32" along a piece of 2x2, and made a pencil mark. Lindsey used the small square to draw a cutting line at the mark.

Sawing

A handsaw cuts when it is pushed down. To begin, place the teeth along the outside of the cutting line. Drag the saw back to make a shallow groove, then push to begin cutting.

Sawing 4x4

Cutting 4x4 is too difficult for most children. The wood fibres will swell up so that even adults will find it easier to make two cuts that join in the middle. For more on sawing, see p. 21.

Safety tips

The "free" end of the wood must never be longer than the supported part.

When you are sawing, your leg should be well to the side of the saw block. Children should move several feet away when the cut is three-quarters done. To protect the floor and prevent the wood from bouncing, you might want to place a folded blanket on the floor where the waste 4x4 will fall.

BIKE RACK

About mitre boxes

A mitre box helps you make perfectly angled cuts, which is important for projects requiring precision or a uniform look.

Clamp as shown, making sure that your board is pressed tightly against the near side of the mitre box. Some mitre boxes have a "lip" that makes it easier to fit against the edge of your work surface.

Sawing with a mitre box

It is easier to start the cut with the saw at an angle, and then straighten it to finish with completely level strokes.

Using 2x2 as a template

Once you have a 32" 2x2, lay it alongside the uncut pieces so you can use it to measure and mark the rest.

5

Lindsey laid the 2x2 across the chairs so that it rested on the mitre box at one end. Dad held the mitre box and 2x2 in place while Lindsey clamped them. Then she slipped a piece of scrap wood under the far end of the 2x2 and clamped those.

6

To start the cut, Lindsey tilted the saw slightly and nicked the corner of the 2x2. As the cut deepened, she lowered the saw so that it was level. When she was finished, they used this piece to measure 19 more; then they clamped and sawed them.

BIKE RACK

7

Dad marked where the nails would go on the ends of two 2x2s. Then he started one nail at each end. He and Lindsey laid the 2x2s across the ends of the 4x4s to form a box. When the corners were matched, Dad hammered one nail at each corner while holding the frame steady.

8

Dad started a second nail at each corner, about 1" from the first. Then they were ready to check whether the frame was square (90°).

Nailing

It is best to have adults "start" the nails (see p. 25): this reduces the chance of pieces of wood shifting while you're trying to nail them together, and also makes it easier for children to hammer straight. Children usually control the hammer better when using both hands, placed fairly far down the handle. If a nail goes in crooked, leave it and go on to the next. When the others are done, remove the crooked nail by hooking the "claw" of the hammer around it and pulling gently. Then try again.

Nail Placement

The first nail should be centred on the 2x2 and about 1" from the end. The second nail, also centred, should go in about 1½" behind the first.

BIKE RACK

Squares and squaring

There are many different sizes and kinds of squares, ranging from try squares to framing squares. Use whichever kind suits your budget and is easy for a child to handle. (Try squares and combination, or set, squares are likely the easiest.)

Measuring tip

For better accuracy when measuring spaces smaller than 1", start your measurements from the 1" mark instead of zero—just remember to add an inch at the end.

9

They held the big square around one corner, and adjusted the frame until it was square. Dad hammered the second nail at one corner, and Lindsey checked one of the other corners to see if it was square. It was, and Dad hammered the other three nails.

10

"Now that the corners are square, we can measure and mark the spacing for each pair of 2x2s," Dad said.

They measured 2½" over for the placement of the second 2x2. That would make the first pair. Then they marked a 5" space before starting the next pair.

11

They followed this pattern for the rest: measuring, marking and nailing the 2x2s until they had ten on the first side. Then Dad carefully turned the frame over so they could nail the second set.

12

Dad and Lindsey spaced each pair of 2x2s so they matched the other side of the rack, and nailed them on. When they were finished, they used 80-grit sandpaper to smooth the worst splintery edges.

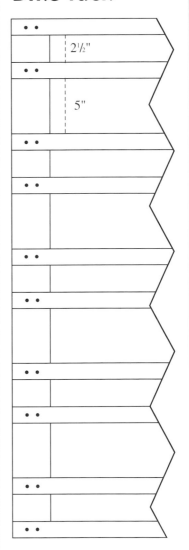

Bike rack

2½"

5"

Tip

The bike rack will be very heavy, so you will need help moving it to its final location.

After the bicycle rack was in place, Lindsey put the front tire of her bike into one of the slots, and the family stepped back to admire it. "No wind is going to knock my bike over now," said Lindsey.

Dad and Mom went in to start dinner. Lindsey and her sister Carly went to find the rest of the family bicycles and filled up the bike rack.

Shelf

Tools and Materials

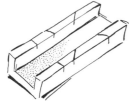

mitre box

sandpaper (80, 100 and 120 grit)

wood glue (white or yellow)

1x4 and 1x6, at least 3' of each; spruce, pine or cedar (we used pine)

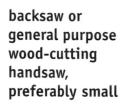

backsaw or general purpose wood-cutting handsaw, preferably small

two pairs strap-on safety goggles (one child-size if available)

try square (or any other square a child can handle; see p. 12)

about 30 finishing nails

five or six large assorted C-clamps (we used two 3", two 4", and two 5")

pencil

tape measure

two dust masks

child's hammer (though a big one will do)

Not shown: Assorted wood scraps to use as saw blocks, cutting guides, clamp pads and sanding blocks (see photos); rags; newspaper (optional); nail set, or nail punch (optional; see p. 31); paint, stain or clear finish (optional).

You will need a traffic-free area; a safe place to put tools and materials when you've finished using them; and a bench, sturdy chair, picnic table, edge of a deck, or other suitable surface. If you are working with long boards, add another support (see photos p. 19).

Most lumberyards use the imperial system of measurement. If you want to use metric, convert our measurements, counting 2.54 centimetres per inch.

Illustrations not to scale

Names for tools can vary. If you are unsure about terms, ask at your local hardware store or lumberyard.

"Lindsey," called Dad, "You have a package from Grandma."

Lindsey opened it and found some books and a letter.

"She says the books are from when you were little, Dad."

"I'd almost forgotten about these," Dad said. "I think you'll really like them."

Mom said, "These books deserve a special place. Why don't you two build a shelf to put them on?"

"Yeah!" said Lindsey.

Dad got some scrap paper and a pencil. He and Lindsey worked on a design together and then went to the lumberyard.

SHELF

About wood

Boards are called "one by six" (1x6), "two by four" (2x4), etc. This refers to the size the board was when it was cut from the log. Smoothing and trimming at the sawmill make it slightly smaller.

Checking for square

Hold the square against the end of the board. If there is a gap between the blade of the square and the edge of the wood, the end isn't square (at a right angle, or 90°).

If the gap is wide, make a new cut to correct the angle. Use your square to draw a new cutting line about 2" from the end of the 1x6. That's enough wood to support the saw while you're cutting.

If the gap is narrow, you can correct it by sanding (see p. 20). For more on squares, see p. 12.

1

"First let's make the shelf top," said Dad. Lindsey chose a piece of 1x6 and checked one end for square. It was too crooked to be fixed by sanding. The other end was just as bad. They would have to cut some wood off one end to correct the angle.

2

There was a knot at the end of the board. "We'll cut that knot off," Dad said. "It would be tough to saw through, and might break out anyway."

Lindsey used the try square to draw a cutting line across the end of the board just past the knot.

SHELF

3

Lindsey set the 1x6 across two sturdy old chairs. Then Dad helped her clamp the board, a cutting guide and a saw block. The cutting guide helped her keep the saw going straight, and the saw block would stop the blade when she was finished the cut.

4

Dad placed the blade of the saw alongside the cutting guide and began sawing the 1x6. Once the cut was started, he and Lindsey worked together to finish it.

Clamping

Clamp the 1x6 to the work surface as shown, using wood scraps as pads to protect the boards from damage by the clamps. Longer boards need support: rest each end on surfaces of similar height, clamping the second support if desired.

Now clamp the cutting guide and the saw block. The cutting guide lies across the end of the 1x6. The saw block lies beside it, *extending past the cutting line*. This will stop the saw when the cut is done. Clamp everything firmly.

Sawing

A handsaw cuts when it is pushed down. To begin, place the teeth along the outside of the cutting line. Drag the saw back to make a shallow groove, then push to begin cutting. Younger children often find it easier to hold the saw with both hands. Lindsey is using one hand with Dad's help and keeping her free hand away from the blade. For more on sawing, see p. 21.

SHELF

Checking for square tip

If you have only a small gap between the board and the blade of the square, you can fix it by sanding (see below).

About sandpaper

Sandpaper comes in various "grits", starting with low numbers for rough sanding to high ones for fine work.

Sanding blocks

When sanding for square, use 80-grit sandpaper, with a sanding block to avoid rounding the end of the board. You can buy sanding blocks, but they are easy to make.

Use a piece of wood that fits easily in your hand. Wrap it in a quarter-sheet of sandpaper, and staple it, if you have a staple gun. The block makes sanding easier.

5

They checked the newly cut end for square. "Great!" Dad said. "That's much better. Now you can measure for the shelf length."

6

Lindsey measured the 1x6 and made a pencil mark 24" from the end they had just squared. She used the try square to draw a straight line across the board at the pencil mark.

SHELF

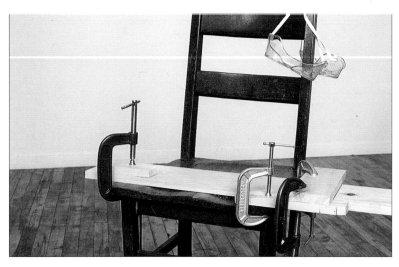

7

Lindsey clamped the 1x6 to a chair. Dad helped clamp on the saw block and the cutting guide.

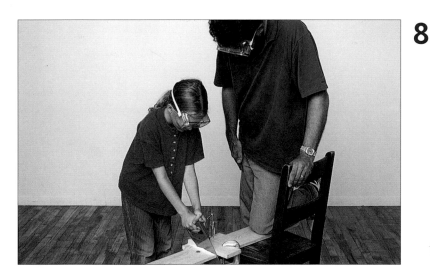

8

Dad started the cut; then Lindsey took over. When she was almost done, Dad went around and held the free end of the board to prevent the wood from breaking. Lindsey checked the cut for square. It was okay.

"There's our shelf top," Dad said.

Clamping tip

If you're using a longer board, you might want to rest the "free" end on a support, or ask someone to hold it. The free end of the board must never be longer than the supported part.

Sawing tips

It's a good idea for an adult to begin the cut and let the child finish. If the child is having difficulty, do the sawing together.

Try to cut with smooth, even strokes, keeping the saw going along the cutting line. Try not to let the saw lean to one side.

Bracing your free hand against the board steadies the work surface, gives you added leverage, and keeps the hand out of trouble.

Holding the saw with both hands can give the younger woodworker more strength and better control.

SHELF

About mitre boxes

A mitre box helps you make perfectly angled cuts, which is important for projects requiring precision.

Clamp as shown, making sure that the board is pressed tightly against the near side of the mitre box. Some mitre boxes have a "lip" that makes it easier to fit against the edge of your work surface.

Clamping tip

Try to place clamps so that they won't trip or poke anyone, or get in the way. If you must place them with the screws upward, watch out for the ends.

Safety tip

Children with long hair should tie it back before starting work.

9

"Now we need to make the brackets and back piece that support the shelf," Dad said.

Lindsey got a piece of 1x4 and checked both ends. Neither was 90°. She made a mark 2" from one end, then used the try square to draw a cutting line at the mark.

10

Dad and Lindsey clamped the 1x4 and the mitre box, matching the cutting line with the correct groove. Lindsey put a piece of scrap wood under the other end of the 1x4 to make it level with the mitre box. Then she clamped both to the second chair.

11

Lindsey knelt so that she could keep the saw level while she was cutting, and held it with both hands. Dad held everything steady while she sawed.

"Now we can cut the brackets and back piece," said Dad.

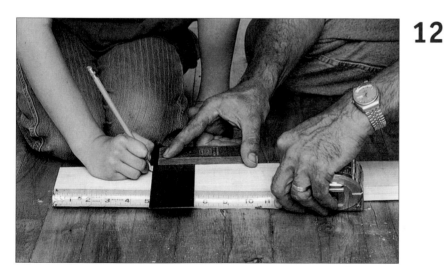

12

Dad and Lindsey measured the 1x4, marking out two 5" brackets and a 20" back piece. They clamped the 1x4 and the mitre box, and cut the first piece. Then they loosened the clamps, moved the board and reclamped it so they could cut another piece.

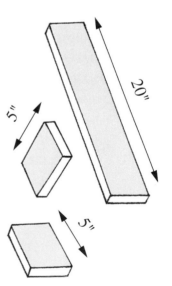

Sawing with a mitre box

It is easier to start the cut with the saw at an angle, and then straighten it to finish with completely level strokes.

Back and bracket pieces

20"

5"

5"

Measuring tip

For better accuracy when measuring spaces smaller than 1", start your measurements from the 1" mark instead of zero—just remember to add an inch at the end.

SHELF

Sanding for smoothness

Start with 80-, move to 100- and finish up with 120-grit sandpaper. Sand in the direction of the grain of the wood. It's a good idea to make one pass with each grit where each side of the board meets. This is called "breaking the corners" and helps to prevent splinters and soften sharp edges.

Safety tip

Hold the sanding block by its top edges; curling your fingers around can lead to scrapes and splinters.

Vertical clamping

The end of the 1x4 must be at a height where the child can, either standing or kneeling, work easily and levelly. To stop the 1x4 from slipping, wedge some scrap wood under the bottom.

13

"We've got all the pieces now, right, Dad?"

"That's right. Now we do some sanding."

Lindsey and Dad used 80-, 100- and then 120-grit sandpaper to smooth the wood and make it look better. Dad wiped the sawdust off when they were done.

14

Now they needed to attach the brackets to the back piece. These pieces would form the base of the shelf. Dad took the back piece and clamped it upright to a chair leg to make nailing on the bracket easier. He adjusted it to a height that would be comfortable for Lindsey.

SHELF

15

To attach the brackets and back, the nails had to go through the brackets and into the end of the back piece (see photo for step 18). Dad and Lindsey figured out where the nails needed to go in and made pencil marks on the brackets.

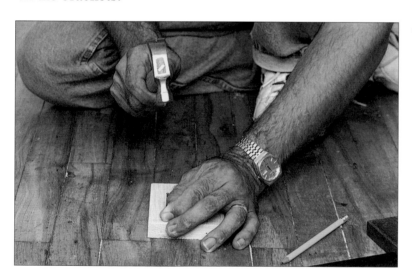

16

Dad started a nail at each of the marks on one bracket. He was careful to keep the nails straight up and down, and tapped them in just enough that they stood firmly on their own. This would make it easier for Lindsey to finish hammering them in.

Marking the back and brackets

Since a piece of 1x4 is actually ³⁄₄" thick, its centre is ³⁄₈" from either edge. Measure ³⁄₈" in from the end of one bracket and make a mark. Now use the try square to draw a straight line across that end. Make two evenly spaced pencil marks along that line, stopping short ³⁄₄" from each edge.

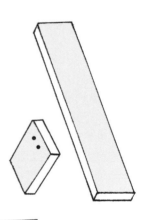

Nailing

See sidebar next page.

SHELF

Gluing tip

Keep a damp rag handy for wiping up spills or blobs, and spread some newspaper if you are worried about your floor.

Nailing

It is best to have adults "start" the nails (see step 16): this reduces the chance of pieces of wood shifting while you're trying to nail them together, and also makes it easier for children to hammer straight. Children usually control the hammer better when using both hands, placed fairly far down the handle. If a nail goes in crooked, leave it and go on to the next. When the others are done, remove the crooked nail by hooking the "claw" of the hammer around it and pulling gently. Then try again.

17

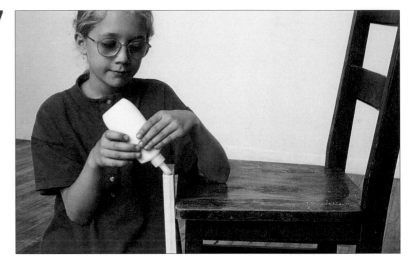

Lindsey put a thin line of glue along the end of the back piece, making sure not to use too much. Then Dad set the edge of the bracket carefully on the end of the back piece, and checked that the two pieces of wood were properly lined up.

18

Dad held the bracket in place while Lindsey hammered in the first nail. When the second nail was well in, he let go and she finished on her own. Then they loosened the clamp and turned the back piece upside-down so they could glue and nail the second bracket.

19

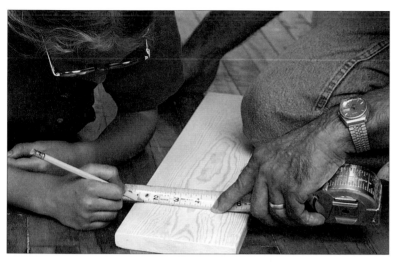

Lindsey used the square to draw two nailing lines across the shelf board, 1⁵⁄₈" from each end. The third line (see above) ran along the back of the board, ³⁄₈" from the edge. For this one they made marks along the board, and used a straight board to draw the line joining them.

20

Dad turned the shelf board over. Then he put the shelf base on top of it. He and Lindsey nudged the base until it was centred between the ends of the shelf board. Lindsey made a pencil mark at the outside edge of each bracket.

Drawing nailing lines

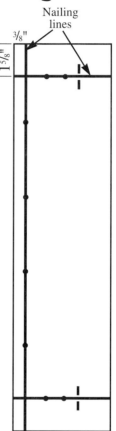

The nails along the back of the shelf go into the back piece, and those across the ends go into the brackets. Space the nails evenly along the lines. The nails going into the brackets must not be placed closer to the edge than 1½", or there is a danger of splitting the wood.

SHELF

Drawing fitting lines

Because you will be nailing "blind", you should double-check your measurements. The nailing lines must be centred over the brackets (³⁄₈" in from the fitting lines). Adjust if necessary.

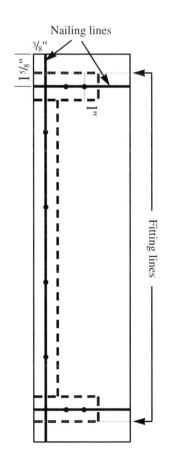

21

Lindsey used the try square to draw a straight line across the shelf board at each of the pencil marks. Dad drew the fitting lines all the way around the board. These would show where the shelf top and the base would fit together.

22

Following the nailing lines, Dad started the nails into the shelf top the same way he started them for nailing the brackets. He kept them straight up and down, and hammered gently until they stood securely upright.

 SHELF

23

Lindsey set the base on the floor and put a thin line of glue along the top edges. Now they had to do the next three steps without stopping, before the glue began to set.

24

Dad set the shelf top onto the base. He carefully aligned the back of the shelf top with the back of the base, at the same time making sure that the outside edges of the brackets matched up with the fitting lines drawn on the shelf board.

Gluing tip

Glue will hold tight joints with a strength equal to that of the wood itself. Place the shelf top on the base, and wipe off any oozing glue before nailing.

About finishes

At this point you might want to start thinking about how you want to decorate the shelf and how you want to hang it. The easiest ways to mount it are to use heavy-duty picture hooks or mounting hardware (available from your local hardware store).

If you would like to use a finish or stain, keep toxicity in mind: water-based finishes, while sometimes a little harder to work with, are much less poisonous and easier to clean up.

25

Dad held the shelf to keep it from tipping. Lindsey hammered a couple of nails along the back of the shelf. She stopped there so that Dad could check the fitting lines (see above) before she hammered the nails into the brackets.

26

Dad turned the shelf sideways to check whether the brackets had shifted (see top). He pushed one bracket over to its fitting line, carefully turned the shelf upright and held the bracket in place while Lindsey hammered the nails. Then they did the same with the other bracket.

27

Lindsey finished hammering the nails. Then she decided that she wanted the nails "set", or sunk below the surface of the wood. Dad used a nail set to do this.

28

"Let's take an eraser and get rid of those pencil lines. Then we'll do some touch-up sanding."

They took turns. When they were done, they wiped the sawdust off.

"The shelf looks great, Dad!"

Setting the nails

A nail set, or nail punch, is a small, inexpensive tool, but somewhat tricky to use. The tip cups the head of the nail, and a hammer is used to tap the other end lightly until the nail is sunk into the wood. (A further option is to fill the holes with wood filler. If you want to use it, follow the instructions on the package.) An easier way to deal with projecting nail heads, however, is simply to gently hammer the nails flat. A few "smiley" marks from the hammer can be a child's badge of achievement!

Touch-up sanding

Use 120-grit sandpaper to put the final touches on your shelf.

"That shelf looks really good," Mom said. "You know, Grandma's birthday is next month. Why don't you two make something for her?"

"I'd love to do that," said Lindsey. "She likes birds. Why don't we make a birdfeeder?"